IT'S A DOG'S LIFE

THE **Footrot Flats**™ SERIES

BY

Murray Ball.

IT'S A DOG'S LIFE

BY

Murray Ball.

ORIN BOOKS

SPLOP!

SCLOP! SCLOP! SCLOP! SCLOP!

I CAN'T BELIEVE IT!
THAT CLUELESS CORGI,
PRINCE CHARLES, HAS WON
A CUP AT THE A&P SHOW!
I MEAN, WHAT WERE THEY
JUDGIN' ON — BELLY STRETCH?

ANYWAY, WHO
CARES!? I'M FIT!
I'M FAST! I'M GOOD
LOOKIN'! WHAT
MORE DO I WANT?

I WANNA
CUP!!

RANGI AND PONGO ARE CAMPIN' OUT FOR THE NIGHT— WAL' HAS COME TO CHECK THEY'RE OKAY. HE'S TELLIN' THEM A BEDTIME STORY...

Murray Ball.

IT'S A BIT SPOOKY...

I THINK HE IS GETTIN' A BIT CARRIED AWAY — HE ALWAYS GOES JUST A BIT TOO FAR...

OKAY, G'NIGHT KIDS, SEE YA IN THE MORNING...

...SWEET DREAMS

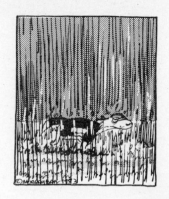

FF/1994

...AND IF YOU'LL JUST KEEP AN EYE ON THE PLACE WHILE I'M AWAY I'LL TAKE THE DOG TO MY BROTHER'S PLACE FOR THE WEEK.

RIGHT

©MURRAYBALL 1984   FF/2025

...IT'LL BE QUITE A TREAT FOR THE DOG— HE'LL MEET HIS MUM.

WOW!

MY MUM!

WHAT A CLASSIC SCENE! THE LONG-LOST SON RUSHES UP THE PATH AND THERE, WIPING HER PAWS ON HER APRON IS HIS DEAR OLD MUM— SHE THROWS WIDE HER ARMS—"HULLO SON!"

"GIDDAY... BOOBSIE..."

Murray Ball.

FF/2030

I MUST SAY I ENJOYED MY STAY WITH WAL'S BROTHER REX THE POT...

I MET MY BLOOD SIRE 'FLASH' AND BOOBSIE, MY MUM. I EVEN MADE FRIENDS WITH REX — HE'S RATHER NICE...

AS A MATTER OF FACT HE GAVE ME A PIECE OF POTTERY...

OH, IT'S A FOOD BOWL... BOWLS HAVE THEIR OWNERS NAME ON THE SIDE — YE GODS, HE WOULDN'T DO THAT TO ME, NOT A NICE BLOKE LIKE REX...

COULD BE WORSE...

BOOBSIE'S RUNT

FF/2206

FF/2207

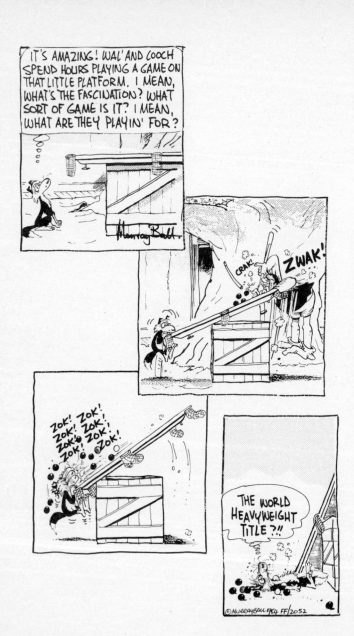

FF/2217

FF/1832

WAL' HAS BUILT THREE GOOD TREE PROTECTORS BUT I CAN TELL HE IS STILL WORRIED THAT THEY WON'T KEEP THAT BLASTED GOAT OUT...

RIP!

FF/2164

WHUMP! WHUMP! WHUMP!

GOOD THINKIN' WAL'.

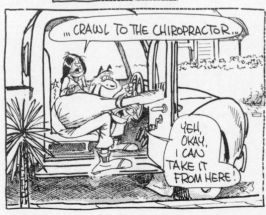

HULLO, MISS WISHART-BETA'S BITCH IS ON THE LOOSE...

I THINK SHE FANCIES ME...

SHE THINKS I'M ROUGH, TOUGH AND MASCULINE!

©MURRAY BALL FBU FF/2053

SCHEHEREZADE, COME HERE THIS INSTANT!

MIND YOU, NEXT TO THE COMPANY SHE KEEPS, SO IS CHRISTOPHER ROBIN'S LITTLE FRIEND, PIGLET...

GOOD GRACIOUS, MISS WISHART-BETA'S SNOOTY BITCH, SCHEHERAZADE IS LOOSE AGAIN...

MurrayBall.

SHE'S GOT A CRUSH ON ME...SHE THINKS I AM TOUGH AND BAWDY—I AM TOO, COMPARED TO TUTANKHAMEN AND POMEROY III, THE ONLY OTHER MALES SHE KNOWS...

GUDDAY 'CURLS— SLUMMING IT AGAIN ARE YOU? Y'NEVER KNOW WHAT SORT OF CRUDE ROUGH-NECK YOU'LL MEET OUT IN THE BUSH HERE...

© MURRAYBALL 1984 FF/2054

SPUT!

BITCH'S BOX

NICE SPITTIN' KID!

© MURRAY BALL 1984 FF/2055

Murray Ball.

AW, LOOK AT THE RIVER MAN! IT'S GOT THE MURPHYS' PIG-MUCK IN IT!

Murray Ball

BY CRIPES, I'LL FIX THAT!

© MURRAY BALL 1984

HEY YOU MURPHY JOKERS, C'MERE YA DIRTY RATBAGS!

HEY WAL', I'VE GOT A WAY TO GET THE RIVER PUT RIGHT...

...BASH THESE JOKERS UP!

THE MURPHY BOYS HAVE COME TO COMPLAIN TO WAL' ABOUT HIM COMPLAINING TO THEM ABOUT THEIR PIG MUCK POLLUTING THE RIVER...

...AND STICK YOUR SNOUT IN AGAIN, FOOTROT, AND WE'LL SET THE DOGS ON YA!

GRROWL! GRUFF!
SNARL! SNAP! GRUFF!
GRUFF!

'SWAT!

WHEN YOUR DOGS CAN HANDLE OUR CAT WE'LL THINK ABOUT LETTIN' THEM HAVE A TRY WITH OUR DOG, EH MURPH'?

SHAKE! SHAKE! SHAKE!

IS THIS WHAT CHRISTMAS HAS BECOME??? AN EXCUSE FOR PROFITEERING, AND SELF-INDULGENCE?

PLASTIC TREES, SYNTHETIC CREAM, ARTIFICIAL COLOURING FROTH AND SYRUP?!!

CHEERS DOG.

RASPBERRY-DROP TEA!!!! MY FAVOURITE!

OH WAL'— MERRY CHRISTMAS!!

H²/10

IT ALWAYS AMAZES ME HOW QUICKLY THE FERVOUR FOR A NEW YEAR'S RESOLUTION WEARS OFF

COOCH RECKONS THE BLACKBERRY IS THE MOTHER OF THE OAK. SO HE'S PLANTED LITTLE OAK TREES UNDER ALL HIS BLACKBERRY PATCHES.

HERE, SHELTERED AND PROTECTED FROM WIND AND PREDATORS IT GROWS UNTIL IT IS STRONG ENOUGH TO FEND FOR ITSELF...

AS A MATTER OF FACT I'VE GOT A SOFT SPOT FOR OLD MUM BLACKBERRY MYSELF.

SNIFF SNIFF

SNIFF

WHO ARE WE? WHY ARE WE HERE? WHAT MAKES US WHAT WE ARE I ASK MYSELF?

© MURRAY BALL 1984 FF/2072

I MEAN, LOOK AT PONGO - SHE'S AN AMBITIOUS KID. IF SHE FAILS TO BREAK INTO THE ARMED FORCES SHE INTENDS FRONTING A RADIO CHAT SHOW

...AND RANGI - HE INTENDS BECOMING A RUGBY PROFESSIONAL - FAILING THAT, MINISTER OF POLICE. I MEAN YOU CAN DO ANYTHING YOU LIKE... THE SKY'S THE LIMIT!

WHY DID I DECIDE TO MUSTER SHEEP, I ASK MYSELF?

...BECAUSE THEY ARE SMALLER THAN ELEPHANTS, I ANSWER.

Murray Ball.

WHAT IS FLAMIN' MAJOR DOIN' HANGIN' ABOUT UNDER MY GIRL'S BITCH'S BOX?

I SHOULD SEE THE CHEEKY SOD OFF— THERE ISN'T ENOUGH ROOM FOR BOTH OF US HERE.

SIGH!

© MURRAY BALL 1984   FF/2180

MAYBE I WAS A BIT RASH TACKLIN' MAJOR TO STOP HIM JUMPIN' UP TO JESS IN THE BITCH'S BOX...

Murray Ball.

HOWEVER THE DIE IS CAST - I HAVE THE TIGER BY THE TAIL AND I SHALL FIGHT TO THE DEATH TO DEFEND JESS' VIRTUE!

YE GODS!

SNAP!

FF/2182

SNAP! SNAP! SNAP! SNAP! SNAP!

SNAP! SNAP! SNAP! SNAP! SNAP!

© MURRAY BALL 84

HOW D'Y FEEL ABOUT CUTTIN' CARDS FOR HER?